TAROT ORIGIN, REVEALED

From Greece to Marseille

Leo Valle

CONTENIDO

INTRODUCTION

When I was reading about the end of the Middle Ages a few years ago, a fact caught my attention. He was one of those characters who do not teach in schools, but his participation in history generated one of the greatest revolutions known, he was the precursor of the Renaissance. This, however, was only the beginning, because when I began to investigate about it, an unexpected idea appeared in my mind. For those unconscious issues that have no explanation, I associated this character with the tarot. When this thought arose I hesitated, but I did what I used to do whenever I doubted, I consulted the cards. To my surprise, they told me that yes, there was a relationship and that if I did enough research I would find it. This is the result of that investigation, I hope it makes you think and you come to your own conclusions. Ultimately, no one has the last word.

ABOUT HISTORY
IN GENERAL

Before going directly into the **history of the Tarot,** I would like to clarify a point in regards to the history in general. This is something I talk about more specifically in other works of my own, so I'll just give a brief overview of it. Basically, we must always take into consideration that what we take for granted in history is nothing more than a theory. No matter how much evidence is presented to support this theory, history is not an exact science and cannot be verified in a laboratory.

There is no way to repeat historical facts to check their authenticity, which is what happens with science. Therefore, unless we discover the time machine to travel to the past and see it with our own eyes, we cannot ensure that things have been as they are taught to us. **History is nothing more than a cultural or social agreement**, which implies that those who have studied this area have agreed to affirm that things were one way and not another. This is how official history is formed, which makes matching pieces fit together and discards the pieces that contradict them, thus forming a consistent theory that denies any evidence that is detrimental to it. The clearest case of this is the **Bible,** which took only 66 books out of the more than 500 that existed in the first centuries of our era.

Not only are there many doubts among researchers about specific historical events, but there are also entire world chronologies totally different from the official one. Suffice it to mention **Newton's Chronology and Fomenko's chronology**, which, centuries apart, both present a very different story from the traditional one. This clarification that I make about history in general, is valid as a context for the history of the Tarot in particular that I will narrate below, which, although it does not contradict the official history and takes it as a basis, presents data that has not been taken into account with previously and that give us a new vision of something that, even, can present us with more surprises.

ABOUT THE ORIGINS OF TAROT

Much can be found about the origin of the tarot, and more with the access to information that the internet allows us, but everything we find will be about contradictory versions in which the most dissimilar origins are raised.

Most coincide with an **Egyptian origin**, but there are those who speak of an **Indian, Chinese, Arab or, of course, gypsy origin**. The reality is that perhaps everyone is partly right. The most logical thing would be to think that the wisdom that the tarot transmits to us cannot be limited to a place, religion or culture. Just as God does not belong to a single religion, but certain cultures had their approach to him at different times and circumstances, giving their own religion characteristics. The same happens with the tarot, it is a universal knowledge that different cultures accessed, giving it its own color or even charm. This is why we can locate their origins in different places and they would not necessarily have to have contact with each other, nor would one be a consequence of the other.

Taking this into account, perhaps it would be best to study each tarot separately, investigating its conception and real influences without trying to link it in a forced way to any previous or simultaneous tarot. I then propose an approach to the most popular and traditional tarot of all, the one whose origin can be traced in a quite verifiable way and, at that point, discover who or who were the inspired or teachers who bequeathed us this wonderful universal method and timeless knowledge. I believe that this study provides us with new, revealing, or even surprising data. This tarot is, of course, **the Marseillaise Tarot**.

The why of the tarot

Before getting fully into the tarot that concerns us, it would be interesting to understand the reason for the existence of this instrument, something that I already outlined in the previous point, but it is worth going a little deeper to fully understand the emergence of the **Marseillaise tarot**.

The answer to this question is so simple that it seems obvious, the existence of the tarot responds to the need of the human being to communicate with the divine. Since primitive man asked the elements of nature to make life easier for him, for it to rain in a drought or to stop raining in a flood, for the sun to rise again after

several cloudy days or for the temperature to rise when winter was very harsh, man always tried to communicate with forces beyond his control. Sometimes asking for help, others trying to identify their signs in order to solve the problems they may have. This human effort to understand or control generated two paths that sometimes went together, many times separated, and many others confused without being able to tell if it was one or the other, these two paths were **science and magic**.

That is why for some people the tarot can be a science, an art or magic. But this is no different from all the methods of divination or spiritual connection that have existed throughout known history. Thus, the desire of man to try to have greater control or knowledge over his life has led him to create systems for acquiring knowledge through communication with invisible forces, which can be deities, disembodied people, spirits of all kinds or simply energy.

That is the reason for the tarot, to communicate with the divinity and, in the case of the tarot that we will deal with, we will be able to see that it was treated in an alternative way to the official one.

THE MARSEILLAISE TAROT

The Marseilles tarot is undoubtedly the most widespread today and is probably the father of most subsequent tarots. These cards date back to the French city of Marseille in 1700, a time when they already appeared in today's configuration, both in terms of the number of cards, their differentiation between minor and major Arcana, and the type of illustrations that are so familiar to us. Now, who were the authors, inventors or creators of this tarot? Nobody knows, there is not a single name that guides us.

What we do know is that Marseille was, from the time we are talking about, an important center for the production of playing cards. In principle, they had the technology, the **printing press** for this time was very widespread and gave the technical possibilities for printing cards. In fact, the Marseillaise tarot is a clear example of a traditional print form, flat colors and a black outline typical of engravings. These cards seem to have been designed to be reproduced on a large scale, and they were.

Although **graphic design** as such did not exist at that time and some printers had unknown but excellent artists, the **Marseille tarot** stands out for its originality and coherence. It is clear that it is not a sum of images but a system designed and carried out with an extraordinary aesthetic and conceptual continuity.

This conforms to one of the most modern theories about the Marseille tarot, that its aesthetic must have been devised by those who knew the most about design at that time, the architects. There are studies on the characteristics of the drawings of each card where specific proportions are found that are repeated or even the use of the number π, issues that undoubtedly point to architectural knowledge. The author of the Marseillaise tarot had not only to be an architect, but also had to have mystical or esoteric knowledge. At that time there was a group in France that had these two characteristics, the **Freemasons**.

It is not necessary in this work to delve into Freemasonry. Suffice it to say that the most accepted theory explains that it was a lodge that arose a few centuries before, originating from the builders of Gothic churches, who kept their construction techniques secret. These societies evolved in the 17th and 18th centuries, on some occasions towards politics and on others towards mysticism, resulting in the latter case, the perfect breeding ground for the **Marseille tarot**.

Although there is no historical data that proves the relationship between freemasonry and tarot, it is not strange that this is the case, we know that we are talking about a **secret society** or at least one individual member of this society that decided to popularize something through the printing press. which was already known in esoteric circles, to this we owe the creation of the marseilles tarot. We know that many of these secret groups were opposed to the power of the church, therefore, to popularize a method of divine consultation, without the clerical intermediary, would be a good blow to the power they were opposed to.

To give data that coincides with this theory, we have the most famous tarot of modern times created two centuries later, the **Rider Waite Tarot**.

In this tarot there is no mystery about its creation, it is known that the author **Arthur Edward Waite** (1857 - 1943) was a well-known freemason, which makes the theory of a freemason author for the Marseille tarot more sustainable. It is also well known that many Masonic schools used the tarot in a ritual or divinatory way, so if the Masons assimilated the tarot into their practices in the 19th and 20th centuries, why not believe that this relationship came from the very beginning of the tarot, or at least the Marseillaise version.

Now, just as what A. E. Waite did was reinterpret an already existing tarot, the Marseillais, the creator(s) of the Marseille tarot, what they did was also reinterpret an already existing tarot, as I said before, which was already handled in the esoteric environments, the **Visconti-Sforza tarot**.

FROM MILAN TO MARSEILLE

At this point, you will already be thinking of a contradiction in what I have been saying. At the beginning I said that it was not necessary to force unions between different tarots and study them separately. However, in the case of these two tarots there is no way to separate them since they are practically the same. They have the same number of cards, the Arcana division and the four suits are the same, and even the illustrations have similar elements. The main difference between one and the other, beyond the two and a half centuries, and the geographical distance that separates them, is aesthetics. While the Marseillaise is about designs made by an unknown person to be printed and disseminated in a more democratic spirit, if you will, the **Visconti Sforza tarot** is a set of miniature works of art made by a well-known artist that were not intended to be mass-produced, but to be a luxury object for the nobility of **Milan.** The socio-cultural transformations of two hundred and fifty years, from the wealthy nobility of the early Renaissance, to the monarchy in crisis of the 1700s, with power struggles behind the scenes, are clearly shown in this evolution of the tarot. From being something for members of a powerful family and their friends, to being something for hundreds of members of a secret society with a desire for expansion.

How the duchy of **Milan tarot got to Marseille** and what happens in those more than two hundred years, remains only in suppositions. We know that **gypsies** have always been the characters most associated with divination by cards, and it is believed that thanks to their nomadic life, the tarot was transferred from one place to another, it is even possible that the tarot has survived the persecution of the church thanks to them. Thus, the theory of the gypsies may be correct, but it is not the only one, and when demonstrating, as we will do next, the origins of the tarot in the nobility of Milan, it is difficult to imagine how this art came to the gypsies.

It happens that in the middle of the 15th century, when the last of the Visconti dukes died without issue, a dispute arose to define who was the legitimate heir to the dukedom. Here appears a famous Frenchman, **Carlos I**, the **Duke of Orleans**, who due to his family ties had full rights to access the dukedom.

This foreign duke, Charles 1, was rejected by local factions, starting a dispute that reached its height in the early 16th century, when the new Duke of Orleans (son of the former and then King Louis XII of France) invaded and occupied the Duchy by force, until after comings and goings, the French were finally expelled in 1521 under the reign of **Francis I**, never to return. Why are we interested in this struggle of the nobility to expand their territories? Precisely because the Visconti-Sforza tarot disappears after this French invasion. It is in this way that although it is not known what treasures of the **Sforza-Visconti** family (last Duke of Milan before the invasion) were stolen by the French, who were ultimately the true heirs, it would not be surprising if a small work of art such as this tarot, has begun its pilgrimage at that

time.

Whether King Louis XII had it in his possession and kept it a secret, or whether it never came into his hands because some French general took it without rendering an account to his superior, for now we do not know. Although this does not explain what happened to the cards until around 1700, when another duke regained the kingdom for the house of Orleans, it is a more likely theory than the one that argues for a random development of the gypsies, in that the nexus it is very clear, the last duke of Milan had the cards, this duchy falls under the French and the cards disappear to reappear later in France.

To all this is added one more piece of information, the **Cary Sheet**, which is a sheet in which there are several tarot cards, very similar to what would later be the Marseille tarot. Little is known about this link that seems to unite the two tarots, but it is believed to be from the 1500s and was made in Italy and then disappeared. It is probable then that not being able to hold on to the original Visconti tarot, some of the French invaders have tried to copy the figures in a much less exquisite way than the model, where the important thing was to preserve the concept of each card and not the artistic expression that represented it.

If this had been the case, there is no doubt that whoever made this reinterpretation of the **Visconti-Sforza** tarot was also a great artist. There is a good chance that the Freemasons did not have

access to the original plates but to a simplified copy, which they made the most of by giving the new figures symbolism typical of the secret association to which they belonged.

Then, the French duke who invaded Milan, kept many of the treasures of the nobility of that territory. Some of the characters close to the duke, who therefore must be someone educated and probably already belonging to some secret society, recognized in that deck something much more transcendental than simple works of art and decided, since it could not be done with them, to make a simplest copy that kept its esoteric meaning. The **Cary plate** could have come from there, but we cannot be sure that this was the case either, since the plate's dating could be doubtful. The fact that this sheet appeared out of nowhere, without any data to indicate where it came from or who made it, means that we must take this curious piece of the puzzle carefully.

Now, what were these cards doing in the **Duchy of Milan**, there is no doubt about that, we know who commissioned them, who made them and, probably, we will discover why.

THE VISCONTI-SFORZA TAROT

Let's continue with a little more history. The Duchy of Milan was created in 1395, Gian Galeazzo Visconti was the first lord of Milan and who gave rise to the dynasty. When the last of the Visconti, Filipo, died without leaving sons in 1447, Milan was declared a Republic, but even so, the succession problems of which we spoke before began. It was Filippo María Visconti who, five years before his death, commissioned the tarot from the artist Bonifacio Bembo, this tarot is known by his name and that of his successor in the dukedom years later, Francisco Sforza. It is believed that this other duke, who had Bembo as the official court painter, could have asked him to make another copy of the deck..

Today several of these cards are kept in different collections that seem to belong to different games. Let us remember that at that time, unlike the Marseilles tarot, each card was a unique work of art, which made its reproduction impossible, the most that could be done was to ask the same or another artist to copy the cards in order to have a second deck. It is probable then that the duke asked for one or more additional decks to give away or to take with him on his travels, which ended up ensuring the survival of this tarot so that today we can be talking about it.

Filippo María Visconti

Filippo (1392 - 1447) is one of the two responsible for this wonderful tarot. It was never thought that he would become Duke of Milan, since apart from not being the firstborn, his health condition, sickly since he was a child, made him, in the eyes of all, incompetent for the position. In fact, it is thanks to his health problems that he was not killed by his own brother, who had already killed his mother, but that Filippo was allowed to live because he did not represent any risk. Young Filippo grew up isolated in a castle in Pavia, confined to protect him from his own illnesses. A small group of people around him took care of his livelihood and education. Among these people were his two tutors, Castellino Beccaria and **Marziano da Tortona**. It is the latter, the fundamental piece to understand the creation of the tarot.

It turns out that Marziano da Tortona, which probably wasn't even his real name, since it belongs to a saint from the first centuries of Christianity, was a known occultist. The practice of changing one's name was something very common at that time, a person without noble lineage but with enough intellectual faculties, to acquire a position at court, plagiarized a famous man so that his name would resonate among the powerful. If we take into account that no one knew anything about history at that time and that few even knew how to read, no one would dispute the identity of a scholar who presented himself with whatever name and credentials. This is one of the great problems of ancient documents, many medieval authors, in order for their work to be known, took names from classical philosophers of whom there was, even by hearsay, some news.

It was then this Marziano de Tortona, who introduced Visconti to esotericism, fostered his interest in mysteries and in the search for metaphysical knowledge. Possibly he helped Filippo achieve the unexpected with his practices, being Duke of Milan, a position in which he would stand out, but which would also allow him to continue delving into esotericism and, finally, leave the world a unique legacy, the tarot.

In fact, there is a deck known as the **Marziano tarot**, which is said to have been the first version commissioned by Visconti and Marziano himself, but it is a reconstruction based on the description given in one of his writings by **Jacopo Antonio Marcello**, a contemporary of Visconti who is known to have had a good relationship with Francesco Sforza, of whom more will be said later. However, there is no other data that certifies the existence of this original tarot, so it is possible that Marcello actually saw a sketch of what the final cards would be. It is possible to think that before the definitive works of art, the artist who made them, **Bonifacio Bembo**, would have made sketches to be approved by Visconti himself.

Bonifacio Bembo

Bonifacio Bembo was a Gothic painter who came from a family of artists. His father was already known before him and his brother was also relatively famous. In fact, the influence of Gothic art can be seen in his cards despite the fact that he had already turned towards Renaissance, being one of the first to do so, which is not a small thing and is consistent with the theory that we are explaining. This change in style, therefore, is not accidental, it was not a matter of fashion, since this new way of seeing the world came from a much deeper philosophy, a philosophy of which the surface or only part of it is barely known. external. Which is reflected in an aesthetic that took elements from the **ancient Greek world.**

Bembo is hired by Visconti as a court artist, a position that he later continued with the duke who succeeded him, Sforza. It is Bonifacio Bembo who designs and produces the first tarot predecessor of the Marseillais that we know today, it is he himself who, at Sforza's request, later makes one or more copies of his own deck. But where does he get his inspiration from, how far did he follow Visconti's instructions and how far are his own ideas?

Again it is necessary to do a little more history. The Renaissance is considered as a cultural and aesthetic movement that happened in Europe, which had art as its maximum testimony, since Renaissance ideas may have been lost in time but art and architecture endure until today and, for many, are the maximum expression of aesthetics that history has bequeathed to us. The point is that if the most visible thing is art, it is not the only thing that this stage left us, the tarot is also an inheritance from that time and is perhaps the most representative expression of the philosophical thought of that time. It is commonly argued that the renaissance began with the fall of Constantinople, when the Greek philosophers of the day went into exile in Florence, taking with them classical thought that had already disappeared for centuries in that region. Well, it was not entirely like that, the Greeks who arrived at that time were well received because a few years ago **Georgios Gemistos Plethon** had traveled to Florence, the true father of the Renaissance and, perhaps, of the tarot.

GEORGIOS GEMISTOS PLETHON

Georgios **Gemistos** is a great unknown to modern culture, he is not studied in schools nor is he someone that ordinary people can talk about. However, in his time he was a great personality, highly respected and internationally recognized. Gemistos was a Greek philosopher who reached 97 years of age, something as unusual at that time as it is today.

He was so respected that even though he did not profess Christianity, he was a

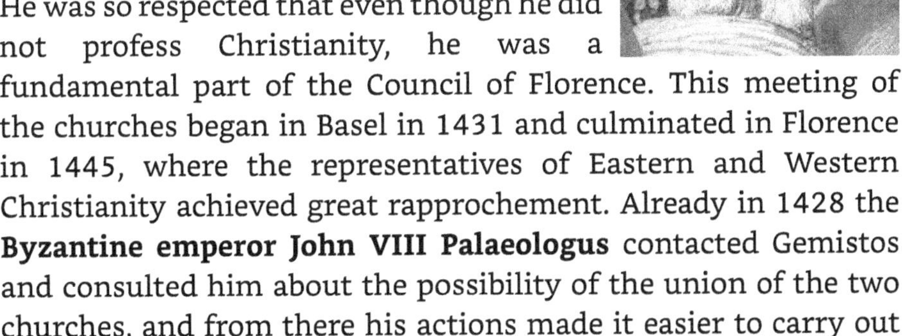

fundamental part of the Council of Florence. This meeting of the churches began in Basel in 1431 and culminated in Florence in 1445, where the representatives of Eastern and Western Christianity achieved great rapprochement. Already in 1428 the **Byzantine emperor John VIII Palaeologus** contacted Gemistos and consulted him about the possibility of the union of the two churches, and from there his actions made it easier to carry out the council.

It is in this way that 25 years before the fall of Constantinople, Georgios Gemistos began to approach the West where he would end up planting with his influence, the seeds of rebirth. This decidedly happened in 1438, when he traveled to Florence with the ecclesiastics from the East to continue the council. Of course, since he was not a Christian, he had a lot of free time during the council, weeks that he took advantage of to teach his doctrine to enthusiastic Fiorentinos, among them **Cosimo de' Medici**, who would later be a friend of Francisco Sforza and his main ally in reaching to become Duke of Milan. But let's not get ahead of ourselves in this sense, because we must continue inquiring about Georgios Gemistos, who is much more than what traditional historians consider, since there are esotericists who recognize him as the incarnation of an ascended master..

The philosophy of Gemistos Plethon

We know that Gemistos was not a Christian, but what was he? It could be said that he was the best representative of the traditional Greek religion or, in any case, of a facet or synthesis of that ancient belief. Although it is difficult for us to think about it today, at that time there were many people who continued to worship the traditional Greek gods, Zeus, Aphrodite, etc. Christianity was a phenomenon established centuries ago that had not completely displaced the gods considered pagan.

Today we have these deities as members of a magnificent

Hellenic literature, but at that time they were still considered real beings who could be talked to and, of course, consulted. We must not forget that the **Greek tradition is full of oracles, in fact, communication with the gods and divination through oracles is a constitutive part of this religion.** Which was of course a threat to Christianity, which did not have this kind of direct communication with the deity, but was based on the interpretation of scriptures, an indirect method. Some of those oracles were very famous, like the one at **Delphi**, and others not so much, like those of the **Orphic sect**, to which Gemistos Plethon is associated.

It is precisely the Orphics who maintained that the true being was the soul, which was reincarnated when the old clothes of the body no longer served. So it is not surprising that his disciples considered **Gemistos** the incarnation of an ascended master, more precisely, **the incarnation of Plato**.

This explains the name by which Gemistos was known, **Plethon,** not to be so obvious, since Christianity was at odds with the concept of reincarnation as much as it is now, but at that time it could be dangerous to admit such a situation. **Plethon** allowed his students to promote this idea, but he never said it, at least not in public. Who better to spread the **Neoplatonism** that generated the renaissance than **Plato** himself?

The man of the oracles

We have already said that the **Orphics** had their oracles, with these they were capable of both understanding philosophical questions and knowing the future, just as the tarot does. But it is not the only source of divination from which Plethon drank. Here things get even more mysterious, because he is known as an initiate in the **Chaldean oracles.** Knowledge that Plethon acquired in his youth from the **Jewish sage Elisha**, a well-known religious and philosophical scholar.

These oracles are texts that date from the first century of our era, channels carried out by a Roman soldier known as **Julian the Theurgist**, but that many attribute directly to **Zoroaster**. The point is that it is affirmed that Neoplatonism had assimilated these texts to its doctrine, and Plethon being considered **Plato** himself, there is no doubt that this affirmation is totally coherent.

is totally coherent.

As if all this were not enough, after passing through Florence, after being repeatedly accused of heresy, it seems that Plethon finished coming clean when he opened his **school of Polytheism**, where he taught the Greek gods, the energy they represented and how to communicate with them. This allowed his influence to continue and he even finished writing his most important works. The fascination that Gemistos Plethon instilled was so great that 12 years after his death in 1454, a controversial Italian figure, **Segismondo Pandolfo Malatesta**, also persecuted by the church, stole Gemistos's remains to take them back to Italy, "so that the great teacher could be found among free men".

After telling you all this, it is easy to understand why nobody talks about **Plethon,** the church censorship tried to erase him from history, so he only appears as a secondary character, when in fact, he was the main philosophical architect of the renaissance.

FROM POLYTHEISM TO TAROT

At this point, the relationship between communication with the gods of Greek polytheism and the tarot is already intuited. Cards already existed in Italy, it was a more or less popular game among the nobility. These cards had images of birds among other things, but they didn't have much to do with tarot.

When **Gemistos Plethon** arrives in Florence and rubs shoulders with the Italian nobility, he no doubt has access to these already existing playing cards. It is not possible to know if it was he who associated one thing with another, what we do know is that after his arrival in Florence, **Bonifacio Bembo** painted the first tarot and, coincidentally, there are those who affirm that he met **Gemistos Plethon** in person.

What many tarot scholars explain is that the trumps originally represented the Greek and Roman gods, in a disguised way to escape the persecution of the church. It is not the objective of this writing to delve into the meaning of the arcana, but as an example we know that **the magician represents Hermes, the moon is Hecate, the emperor is Zeus, the force is Hercules** and so on with the rest of the cards. I recommend to those who are interested in this subject, that they look for literature on the matter since it exists and it is highly recommended.

The influence of the pagan sage **Plethon** transformed the thinking of the Italian nobility, who, in constant conflict with the power of the church and its authority over the spiritual and earthly life of men, decided to return to their non-Christian origins and communicate with the gods without intermediaries. **Filipo Visconti** in conjunction with Bonifacio Bembo, were the ones who took the definitive step, **Visconti's mystical** search together with **Bembo's knowledge** and artistic talent, both inspired by **Plethon's philosophy**, which brought them closer to a glorious classical past, resulted in this inspired and first tarot.

The definitive role of Sforza

It is then that the figure of Francisco Sforza appears, who without being from the nobility, acquires the title of duke granted by the Senate of the Republic of Milan, determining the end of the republic and the beginning of the Sforza dynasty. To reach this position, not only did he need to marry Bianca María Visconti, but he also resorted to all kinds of resources, from alliances to betrayals with all the neighboring fiefdoms of the time and, I don't know, he shouldn't let it go, that his friendship with the **Médiccis** made things easier for him. The relationship between Sforza and the artist Bembo, who made a famous portrait of the duke from which we know his physiognomy, may have gone deeper than simple patronage. Both **Francisco Sforza** and the artist **Bonifacio Bembo** seem to have belonged to a select group that had certain esoteric knowledge. Societies were very common back then and Sforza belonged to several of them. For example, he was a member of **the order of the Knight of the Crescent** along with Jacopo Antonio Marcello, of whom I have already spoken before.

Sforza's relationship with the **Médiccis,** who were the ones who welcomed **Gemistos Plethon** at the time, and Bembo's own relationship with Plethon close the circle. It is **Francisco Sforza** who achieves that the tarot does not die with the previous duke. Either because he knew the importance and used this divinatory method, or simply to look good and give precious gifts to his noble friends affirming his commitment to pagan thought, Sforza asks Bembo for replicas of his own work. This means that the tarot is not lost and there are still traces of these original decks in different art collections.

IN SUMMARY

The well-known **Marseillaise tarot** has its origins in the first **Visconti-Sforza tarot**, and this arose from the mysticism and oracular philosophy brought from Greece by **Gemistos Plethón**, for whom communication with the deities was a fundamental part of their tradition. The cards used as a game in feudal Italy, merged with the Greek deities and their Roman correspondences that had already been forgotten in the peninsula, but thanks to the Neoplatonism of Gemistos that gave rise to the Renaissance, came back to life in clear opposition to the Roman Church, whose power was a nuisance to rising feudal lords. These old but new deities must have been hidden in the oracle deck, since this opposition to the church could not be open or evident, but it was something in which many nobles agreed, making the tarot an ideal means to confront the monopoly of God that held Catholicism.

It is in this way that the pagan beliefs of a limited group of nobles in Italy centuries later, together with the revolutionary ideas of France and the advent of the printing press, became the most popular means of consulting the deity without the dogmatic intermediary of the official religion.

This new popular oracle was the trigger that made modern fortune tellers prosper, which multiplied by thousands, since the new tarot tool made more accessible to all what in Delphi and other Greek cities was the power of a few, fluid communication With God.

IN CONTACT

I thank you dear reader that you have come this far and I invite you to review my catalog on Amazon with other books of my authorship.

You can find me on my YouTube channel: Leo el observador.
You can also write to my email: tarotarkiel@gmail.com

ABOUT THE AUTHOR

Leo Valle

Acerca del autor Leonardo Valle Leo Valle has written on different topics ranging from historical research to fiction. In the nineties he directed a magazine on alternative disciplines and spirituality called "Volvamos al Sol", which led him to investigate different aspects of esotericism and travel to India. Simultaneously, his passion for fiction led him to write different works, among which "Navarro" stands out, a historical novel that won the first prize for the Young Argentine Novel in 2005. Today he continues to transition between these two genres and prepares several titles for the coming years.